To Jim + Ingrid with love Alison +
Patrick
Xmas '94

CW01637206

EXCUSE MY CLERIHEWS

Lamented Eve:
'Oh! Adam, it's hard to believe
we made such a ghastly mistake
after chatting to that snake.'

Illustration by Jacqui Hazell

EXCUSE MY CLERIHEWS

by

WILLIAM HAZELL

William Hazell

Hampus Books

First published in Great Britain by
Hampus Books
PO Box 227
Folkestone
Kent CT20 1GB

Printed in Great Britain by
RB Print
Unit 13, Highfield Industrial Estate
Folkestone
Kent CT19 6DD

British Library Cataloguing in Publication Data.
A catalogue record for this book is
available from the British Library.

ISBN 0 9523298 0 8

For
MADELEINE ROCHAT
with love

Contents

Acknowledgements

I wish to express my warm thanks to Sir Stephen Spender for his kindness and encouragement;

to Mrs Clare Douglas who, long ago, introduced me to the delights of Bentley's clerihews;

to Mr Wes Magee who was the first to discern some slight promise in my own nonsense verse;

to Mr Gavin Ewart for persuading me not to give up writing clerihews even when no-one would publish them;

and to Mr C.F. Orman for his patient ear and many constructive suggestions.

W.H.

CORRIGENDUM

Page 65, last line:
For Brummel please read Brummell.

The Rhymer's Exhortation to the Public

The late Edmund Clerihew Bentley
studied History intently,
and published much sensitive data
which established his fame as an Eminent Educator.

The Present Writer
similarly is a fighter
for the wider dissemination
of hitherto strictly privileged information.

To be aware that Isaiah
invented the tumble dryer,
and that Cromwell was really a woman,
advances our understanding of what is human;

While to know that Bach wrote his cantatas
on a diet of chipolatas
can only enhance our ability
to grasp the relevance of nutrition to creativity.

At a time when Mr Major
is increasingly showing signs of disturbed behaviour,
it behoves us all to do our best to subserve
the socio-economic system in which we swerve.

What better method, then, to help the economy
(while not forgetting the warnings in Deuteronomy)
than by trying our utmost to follow historic example
(except, of course, where doing so might be harmful).

This Work therefore aims to remind the people of Britain
how the heroic men and women of whom I have written,
in lives (like our own) so often troubled or tiring,
accomplished results which are seldom less than inspiring.

A

Although the High Priest Aaron
had a day of silent prayer on,
he sportingly undertook
to inaugurate this book.

* * *

Ms Kate Adie
is a famous newshawk lady.
She's one of the ace newsfalcons
reporting from the Balkans.

* * *

Aesop
slaved in a teashop.
He made up his fables
while laying the tables.

* * *

It was Marcus Vipsanius Agrippa
who invented the zipper
to assist in removing his toga
for doing yoga.

* * *

The Emperor Akbar
would happily lunch at a snack bar.
When he was in a hurry
he took away takeaway curry.

* * *

The Pharaoh Akhenaten
built pyramids out of carton,
then sent Queen Nefertiti
to live in Cardboard City.

* * *

Alcibiades
often wept as he gazed at the Pleiades.
When Socrates asked him why,
a sob was his only reply.

* * *

Louisa May Alcott
lay awake in her small cot
and prayed she'd put nothing too grim in
Little Women.

* * *

President Idi Amin
sent the following note to the Queen:
'Have just won the DBE.
Yours, Amin, VC, PTO, DSO, MC.'

* * *

St Thomas Aquinas
had trouble with his sinus.
Such was his apology
for writing theology.

* * *

The largesse of Fatty Arbuckle
was remarkable.
He once gave a dollar
to Fats Waller.

* * *

When W.H.Auden
was surrounded by a police cordon,
he sat down in the street
and counted feet.

* * *

The Canterbury St Augustine
is the one *I* trust in.
St Augustine of Hippo was a hippy,
and slightly dippy.

*
* *

B

I can't say if the Emperor Babar
ever voted Labour,
but he once told a pollster from Mori
that he wouldn't be voting Tory.

* * *

To believe that Sir Francis Bacon
could have undertaken
the Works of our Loftiest Bard
is soft - and, for others, hard.

* * *

Lord Baden-Powell
belatedly wooed a Brown Owl,
but, finding her too scrawny,
forsook her for a Tawny.

* * *

'I don't hold with Hard Rock,'
said Béla Bartók.
'Neither do I,'
said Zoltán Kodály.

* * *

Sir Arnold Bax
was devoted to yaks
and is best known for his charming 'Tibet
Quintet'.

* * *

Mrs Annie Besant
received a nice present
of candy
from Gandhi.

* * *

When Queen Boadicea
saw a Mexican with a tortilla,
she offered to carry it
in her chariot.

* * *

Benjamin Britten
was painfully bitten
on the ears
by Peter Pears.

* * *

It is said that Edmund Burke
went totally berserk
when a goat had several tastings
of his notes on Warren Hastings.

* * *

When Byron
put a spare tyre on,
he shed a bitter tear
and wrote 'On This Day I Complete My Thirty-
Sixth Year.'

*
* *

C

John and Sebastian Cabot
were creatures of habit.
Be it never so boring,
they just couldn't help exploring.

* * *

Julius Caesar
didn't get a visa
to visit Kent.
He just went.

* * *

Cain and Abel
tanked up on Black Label.
Then Cain went to gaol
and drank Adam's ale.

* * *

Far be it from me to condone
the transgressions of Al Capone,
but at least in his rather brash way
he remembered St Valentine's Day.

* * *

Truman Capote
never wore a dhoti,
not even in India.
He said, 'It would be a sin, dear.'

* * *

In winter, Archbishop Carey
found it rather scary
every time Lord Coggan
flashed by on a toboggan.

* * *

Sir Roger Casement
declined to lodge in a basement,
but was quite ecstatic
when offered an attic.

* * *

Catullus
always screamed when he saw a portcullis.
Perversely, he never made scenes
when he saw guillotines.

* * *

Poor Coco Chanel!
When 1 to 4 didn't sell
she somehow had to survive
on No.5.

* * *

The Emperor Charlemagne
was insanely fond of champagne.
Whenever he went to a parley
he was hailed as Champagne Charlie.

* * *

Cleopatra
was placed under a *fatwa*
by the Iranians
for cohabiting with aliens.

* * *

King Clovis
refused to eat Hovis.
What he usually ate
was a baguette.

* * *

King Croesus
published a treatise
(which the Lydians were feverishly buying)
entitled *How to Be Rich Without Really Trying*.

* * *

One would have thought that St Cyril's
extraordinary affinity with squirrels
should have made him their patron saint;
but he ain't.

*
* *

D

It was heedless
of Daedalus
not to have been more rigorous
with Icarus.

* * *

Salvador Dali
always wrote his cheques in Pali.
He considered it an ill omen
if he got a bill written in Roman.

* * *

Dante
was the eternal dilettante.
Though his motives were the purest,
he only went to the Inferno as a tourist.

* * *

This, I suspect, was the favourite
epitaph of King David:
Here lieth
Goliath.

* * *

Delacroix
cried, *'Vive le Roi!'* –
then in a fit of pique
shouted, *'Vive la République!'*

* * *

Perhaps, to be fair, Delilah
had ambitions as a hairstyler
and saw Samson as a skinhead,
not dead.

* * *

In Brussels,
flexing his muscles,
Jacques Delors
asked for more.

* * *

Dame Judi Dench
speaks almost perfect French.
She once said to René Clair:
'Comment allez-vous, mein Herr?'

* * *

'The fascinating thing
about Deng Xiaoping
is his diminutive stature,'
said Mrs Thatcher.

* * *

Descartes
didn't know much about Art,
but knew that he didn't like
Vandyke.

* * *

Sew-sew Christian Dior
was a chauvinist pig to the core.
When women answered back
he put them in a sack.

* * *

Sir Francis Drake,
when offered a piece of cake,
said he wouldn't risk it,
and took a ship's biscuit.

*
* *

E

Prayed Mary Baker Eddy:
'O Lord, mayst Thou soon be ready
to place Thy whole reliance
on Christian Science.'

* * *

Thomas Alva Edison
swallowed his last dose of medicine
and expired at eighty-four,
complaining about the phonograph next door.

* * *

Edward, the Black Prince,
often pined for a shampoo and rinse;
yet he was not at all dressy,
and fought like a lion at Crécy.

* * *

In North Africa, General Eisenhower
once got up at five (long before his regular rising hour)
to check that General Patton
had remembered to let the cat in.

* * *

Sir Edward Elgar
kept his manuscripts under a bell jar
to prevent them becoming musty
and getting dusty.

* * *

El Greco
didn't go for Art Deco.
He owed his very survival
to Greek Revival.

* * *

Epicurus
was not as pure as
Epictetus,
nor as neat as.

* * *

Erasmus
was quite convinced that miasmas
rising from tropical jungles
were the reason for Luther's theological bungles.

* * *

Ethelred the Unready
when drunk became very unsteady,
and had to be put to bed
complaining, 'Oh, my head!'

* * *

Prince Eugene's
blue jeans
and Marlborough's denim
became all the rage after Blenheim.

* * *

It is questionable if Euripides
knew much about the flora of the Antipodes.
I fear he slipped up when he mentioned the azalea
in his *Iphigenia in Australia*.

* * *

Lamented Eve:
'Oh! Adam, it's hard to believe
we made such a ghastly mistake
after chatting to that snake.'

*
* *

F

When Gabriel Fahrenheit
was rescued on a cold day from a barren height,
there was little they could do.
He was only thirty-two.

* * *

General Fairfax
considered the bare facts
(not without self-loathing)
when the enemy captured his clothing.

* * *

'Hiya!'
cried Manuel de Falla
to Joaquín Rodrigo,
who replied, 'I don't speak American, *amigo.*'

* * *

'A bird in the hand,'
said King Ferdinand,
'is worth two in the bush, Isabella.
I think you're investing too much in this Columbus fella.'

* * *

Millard Fillmore,
you may be still more
indifferent to learn than I am to convey,
was thirteenth President of the USA.

* * *

A fetishist, Flaubert
loved to caress mohair.
He confessed that he only wrote
to get someone's goat.

* * *

Errol Flynn
had great confidence in skin.
He said, 'What I want to affirm is
my faith in the epidermis.'

* * *

Marshal Foch
had no time at all for the Boche.
He flatly refused to catch diesels
or German measles.

*
* *

G

Of course, it was reckoned a scandal
when George the Second told Handel
he enjoyed *The Royal Fireworks*
more than his Higher Works.

* * *

Sitters for Giacometti
had to be as thin as spaghetti.
Models with tapeworms
got special terms.

* * *

André Gide
had a thing about Ganymede.
He was always seeking his double.
It gave him no end of trouble.

* * *

The great Giotto
practically lived on risotto
when he was painting a fresco.
He generally got it from Tesco.

* * *

Gossip has it that Glinka
once called Scriabin a stinker,
and was even more horrid in
a remark he made about Borodin.

* * *

Dr Goebbels
got hiccups and stomach burbles
when, with typical lack of candour,
he swallowed his own propaganda.

* * *

When he found Johann Wolfgang von Goethe
lunching on a frankfurter,
Johann Christoph von Schiller
said *that* wasn't much of a filler.

* * *

Maxim Gorky
kept a parrot called Squawky
which was banished to Sakhalin
for screeching, '*Down with Stalin!*'

* * *

After painting *that* portrait, Goya
got a stiff letter from the Duke's lawyer.
As for the Duchess,
she spent six months on crutches.

* * *

I can't
say if General Grant
drank Haig. As to whether General Haig
drank Grant's, I'm just as vague.

* * *

That Gustavus Adolphus
was one of Sweden's worst golfers,
historians see fit to ignore
when discussing the Thirty Years' War.

*
* *

H

At St Andrews, where Haile Selassie
was golfing with Vincent Massey,
a deferential caddie
addressed him as Highly Sir Laddie.

* * *

King Hammurabi
won the first Derby
with Babylon
at 6 to 1 on.

* * *

The Caliph Harun al-Rashid
found his pampered life too placid
till Allah opened his eyes
to blessings in disguise.

* * *

Admittedly Lord Healey
is abysmal at Matabele,
but happily his French is
as brilliant as Judi Dench's. *

* * *

For Helen of Troy
going to Paris brought little joy.
Though she launched a thousand shops,
they were all flops.

* * *

The garb of Hengist and Horsa
could hardly have been coarser.
They had no substitute
for jute.

* * *

Henri III
mangeait des petits pois
avec son couteau.
Ce n'est pas comme il faut.

* * *

* Dame Judi Dench (q.v.)

Hereward the Wake
was something of a fake.
When he lived in the Fens
he never once awoke before the hens.

* * *

That Thomas Hobbes
wrote a treatise on thingumabobs
is all I can recall.
Yes, that's about all.

* * *

It's a pity that David Hockney
is such a rabid cockney.
An artist invites severe strictures
when he asks, ' 'ow d'yer like these 'ere pickchers?'

* * *

Oliver Wendell Holmes
wouldn't tolerate heavy tomes
at the Breakfast Table.
They had to be read in the stable.

*
* *

I

When St Ignatius Loyola
condemned *Pepsi*- but not *Coca*-Cola,
was he being hypocritical
or simply jesuitical?

* * *

The indifference of Washington Irving
to the Church of Rome was disturbing.
When asked if he'd heard of the Pope,
he answered, 'Nope!'

* * *

Sensible Queen Isabella
always took an umbrella
whenever she went to the plain
during her reign in Spain.

* * *

Christopher Isherwood,
as any judicious Britisher would,
preferred *pre*-Hitler Berlin
as a city in which to sin.

* * *

'Don't give me that Jerry bull!'
thundered Ivan the Terrible
when a half-petrified Prussian
tried to pass himself off as a Russian.

*
* *

J

Jael
knocked a nail
into the pate of Sisera
because she hated his viscera.

* * *

Because St James the Less
had so obviously failed to impress,
he always felt rather sore
with St James the More.

* * *

Even though Henry James
was a hopeless duffer at games,
he loved playing shuffleboard
with Mrs Humphry Ward.

* * *

Nothing provoked the ire
of the Prophet Jeremiah
quite so much as to hear folks say,
'Have a nice day!'

* * *

St Jerome K. Jerome,
to the great confusion of Rome,
produced the Vulgate, then wrote
Three Men in a Boat.

* * *

Jezebel asked Elijah
if he would oblige her
by calling a minicab
for King Ahab.

* * *

I am sorry to say that Jonah
was an incorrigible moaner,
and could never resist telling tales
about whales.

* * *

King Josiah of Judah
didn't like mock-Tudor.
He built his domicile
in the Neo-Gothic style.

* * *

King Juan Carlos
suffered a bizarre loss
when Queen Sophia
said, 'Lend me your ear!'

*
* *

K

'Don't bother to send for the police,'
said President Karamanlis
when Colonel Papadopoulos
hurled himself (à la Tosca) from the Acropolis.

* * *

Rudyard Kipling
once bludgeoned a stripling
for speaking ill
of *Puck of Pook's Hill.*

* * *

Even when Lord Kitchener
had anitchina
nawkward place,
he never relaxed his face.

* * *

John Knox
always studied people's socks.
That was his criterion
for judging a Presbyterian.

* * *

'What time does the bus go?'
asked General Kościusko.
'I don't want to miss my attendance
at the American War of Independence.'

* * *

Prince Peter Kropotkin
toured Europe with a bodkin,
looking for Heads of State
to assassinate.

*
* *

L

How beautiful are the lines of Lamartine:
'Ah! Martine
Navratilova,
move over. . .'

* * *

Walter Savage Landor –
never one to pander –
liked to quarrel and rebel.
But he wrote a nice farewell.

* * *

Sir Harry Lauder
was a legend north of the Border.
He was said to be very well built
under his kilt.

* * *

Mr Lee Kuan Yew
wouldn't harm an old man with a queue,
but he barbered *young* men with long hair.
Ye gods, he was a square!

* * *

Admitted Leibnitz:
'When I've been imbib'n', it's
a job to tell monads
from gonads.'

* * *

When the Earl of Leicester
whispered that the Queen wore polyester,
Sir Francis Bacon
swore he must be mistaken.

* * *

Ruggiero Leoncavallo
was liverish and sallow.
He frequently lost his rag
with people who called *I Pagliacci* 'Pag'.

* * *

When I asked Martyn Lewis,
'Do you know what a clerihew is?'
he said, 'Give me one or two clues –
but tell me, is it good news?'

* * *

Fra Filippo Lippi,
when the nights were turning nippy,
would shrink into his cowl
and emit a high-pitched howl.

* * *

When ladies used to insist
on kissing the Abbé Liszt,
he never displayed any wrath,
despite being a man of the cloth.

* * *

Lloyd George
never knew Boy George.
I expect he would rather
have known his father.

* * *

John Locke
suffered a terrible shock
when his *Essay Concerning Human Understanding*
was left out for the dustman, on the landing.

* * *

'You've got the wrong fellow!'
protested Longfellow.
It gave him a lot of bother
being mistaken for Hiawatha.

* * *

Though Lot
quite plainly was not
in a fit state to do it,
he chipped off a bit of his wife to put in the cruet.

* * *

The mad King Ludwig
(once called by Dr Spooner 'the lad-king Mudwig')
was ruler of Bavaria,
a distinctly loony area.

* * *

Few men's foes were uncouther
than those of Martin Luther.
One's inside fairly squirms
at the thought of their Diet of Worms.

*
* *

M

The Rt. Hon. Harold Macmillan
thought ex-President Juan Perón was a villain,
but was far too well-mannered to say so,
and tipped him a peso.

* * *

Salvador de Madariaga
dreamed of being dressed by Balenciaga.
Such fancies were also a facet
of José Ortega y Gasset.

* * *

An animal-lover, Gustav Mahler
wrote *Ich ging mit Lust** for an impala,
while *Die zwei blauen Augen von meinem Schatz***
was inscribed to the most pampered of his cats.

* * *

While, to us, Mr John Major
may seem just a grey middle-ager,
he is probably seen in a warmer
light by Norma.

* * *

Dr Malan
was not a tolerant man.
He hated the guts
of General Smuts.

* * *

André Malraux
was always on the go.
He could even go daringly far,
as when he said *'Merde!'* to the Shah.

* * *

* 'I went with desire.'
** 'The two blue eyes of my treasure.'

That the famous Duke of Marlborough
frequently visited Aldeburgh
one learns from *The Life and Times
of Peter Grimes.*

* * *

When Mary, Queen of Scots,
came out in spots,
Lord Darnley
regarded her wanly.

* * *

W. Somerset Maugham
sometimes wrote in cuneiform.
When he wished to be more specific
he wrote in hieroglyphic.

* * *

Sir Yehudi Menuhin
is absolutely genuine.
There is certainly nothing phoney
about his interpretation of Albinoni.

* * *

Sir Robert Menzies
was the victim of terrible frenzies
in which he would sob, 'I'm a failure!
Why am I only Prime Minister of Australia?'

* * *

Why did Gerardus Mercator
have to spread such a canard about the Equator?
Perhaps he thought it droll
to make it look no longer than a Pole?

* * *

Mies van der Rohe
adored being squeezed by his boa.
He kept it in the cowhouse.
It wasn't allowed in the Bauhaus.

* * *

A.A.Milne
baked Winnie the Pooh in a kiln,
then became a millionaire
with 'Anthony Wedgwood Bear'.

* * *

Field Marshal Montgomerwy
wouldn't tolerwate flummerwy.
When his cook compared him to Caesar
he put her in the fweezer.

* * *

Moses
adopted one of his poses
when he stood with Aaron
to be photographed on the perron.

* * *

Mussolini
washed his mouth in Martini.
He made Count Ciano
gargle with Cinzano.

*
* *

N

Napoleon Bonaparte
never took a loan, apart
from borrowing half the pay
of Marshal Ney.

* * *

John Nash
said, 'I'm just off to a bash.
If anybody 'phones
say I'm in consultation with Inigo Jones.'

* * *

King Nebuchadnezzar
stored in his wordprocessor
as much as he could recall
of the Writing on the Wall.

* * *

The peevish tones of Noah
crackled over the blower:
'Could we please have less snorting and squeaking?
This is your captain speaking.'

* * *

Nostradamus
never bought pyjamas.
He thought it pleased the Almighty
to see him in a nightie.

*
* *

O

Oedipus
adopted a somewhat seedy puss
which, having lost its tom-sex,
had a Needy-puss complex.

* * *

King Offa
bought everything he saw on 'special offer'.
Any offers he didn't like
were tossed over Offa's Dyke.

* * *

King Og
was the first man to jog.
He jogged all over Bashan.
It was his passion.

* * *

Georg Simon Ohm,
trying to teach his wife about Current on the bus home,
was unable to instruct her
owing to the resistance of the conductor.

* * *

In a horrible nightmare, Onassis
saw dollars and diamonds in masses
crossing the oceans in argosies –
all Niarchos's . . . !

* * *

Would *you* have thought George Orwell
foresaw 1984 well?
Why, he couldn't even foresee
1983.

*
* *

P

Milan Panič*
doesn't speak any Spanič.
He's even rather slow at
Serbo-Croat.

* * *

Pepin the Short
was a jolly decent sort.
He always gave Charles Martel
cognac for Noël.

* * *

* A Serbian-American businessman, he was briefly Prime Minister of Jugoslavia in 1992.

Phidias
wouldn't sculpt anything hideous.
The mere thought of having a sitter over thirty
was enough to make him shirty.

* * *

In her modest Left Bank apartment, Édith Piaf
kept a large pet giraffe.
There were problems, such as shutting the *fenêtre,*
etc.

* * *

No President was less fierce
than Franklin Pierce.
Even Benjamin Harrison
was a terror by comparison.

* * *

Piero della Francesca
never read Arnold Wesker.
If he had, I still don't think
he'd have painted the kitchen sink.

* * *

Lester Piggott
is not a bigot.
He doesn't criticize sinners
who've never ridden winners.

* * *

Pindar
had too many Kinder,
so he sent them to a Spartan-
garten.

* * *

Plato
opposed Athens joining NATO.
He couldn't stand the Yanks'
think-tanks.

* * *

It's quite true that Pocahontas
flew Qantas,
but probably only a myth
that the pilot was Captain John Smith.

* * *

President James K. Polk
would never say 'okey-doke'
or 'crap' or 'the whole shebang'.
He *hated* slang.

* * *

Sir Carl Popper
disdained to wear a topper,
and his taste was far too simple
to consider a wimple.

* * *

'What I write *isn't* beastly!'
insisted J.B.Priestley.
He denied that *Angel Pavement*
incited lust and depravement.

* * *

'Prinny'
didn't care for his friends to be skinny.
He preferred someone he could pummel –
like Beau Brummel.

* * *

The memories of Proust
all came home to roost.
The process was begun
when he ate a bun.

* * *

Puccini
was very much affected by Rossini.
The Barber of Seville
made him ill.

* * *

'These ideas of young Pythagoras,'
declared his tutors, 'simply stagger us!
We just cannot share his views
about the square on the hypoteneuse.'

*
* *

Q

Is the speling of Dan Quayle
really beyond the pail?
After all, we cannot be certain that even Plato
was able to spell 'potatoe'.

* * *

'Thanks a million!!!'
raved the great teacher Quintilian.
He was famed for his frank ebullition
when receiving fees for tuition.

*
* *

R

'So you play Scrabble, eh?'
gasped Rabelais,
marvelling at the brain
of ten-year-old Montaigne.

* * *

Field Marshal Count Radetzky's
astounding campaign on jet-skis,
although in its day much lauded,
has not previously been recorded.

* * *

The thing that baffles
about Sir Stamford Raffles
is what on earth he saw
in Singapore.

* * *

Sir Walter Raleigh,
as a sort of finale
to laying down his cloak,
offered his Queen a smoke.

* * *

Few pharaohs were as fecund
as Rameses the Second.
His children numbered a hundred.
How lucky their education was state-funded!

* * *

President Ronald Reagan
ran amok with a spray-gun,
painting goofy graffiti
all over New York City.

* * *

Lord Reith
wailed and gnashed his teeth
when paying his licence fee
to the BBC.

* * *

FDR
never slept with a superstar.
He was more restrained in this way
than JFK.

* * *

Rossini
had certain reservations about Puccini.
His comment after hearing *La Bohème*
was . . . 'Ahem!'

* * *

When Mstislav Rostropovich's
tickets were switched with Dmitri Shostakovich's,
the airline sent an apology
but explained that its staff were not trained in musicology.

* * *

Sir Peter Paul Rubens
seldom painted lupins.
He preferred inspirational lines,
like *The Rape of the Sabines.*

* * *

Bertrand Russell
didn't have much muscle,
but remained very wiry
until his expiry.

*
* *

S

The Marquis de Sade
whipped satisfyingly hard
when von Sacher-Masoch
prostrated himself on a hassock.

* * *

George Santayana
swung on a liana
while he rested for a season
from *The Life of Reason*.

* * *

The Assyrian King Sargon
had no patience with fancy jargon.
Nothing, he thought, could be phonier
than the way those hippies talked in Babylonia.

* * *

Andrea del Sarto's
Adam Picking Tomatoes
played a significant part
in the development of Social Realist Art.

* * *

Schiaparelli's
shocking pink wellies
sold like hot cakes.
She supplied them to several sheikhs.

* * *

Skanderbeg
liked to go to work on an egg.
One morning his egg broke down
and he had to take a sausage into town.

* * *

Socrates
was tolerant of handsome mediocrities.
Any willing ephebe with a modicum of nous
was welcome in his house.*

* * *

From his childhood Frederick Soddy
intended to be a Somebody.
He lived in the highest hopes
of discovering isotopes.

* * *

Initially, King Solomon
made his name with a column on
the Wisdom of Israel
in the *Daily Mail.*

* * *

Solon
scorned to use a full stop or a colon.
His only punctuation was a dash –
no wonder his reforms were such a hash.

* * *

* When his wife Xanthippe (q.v.) was away.

The conducting of Sir Georg Solti
is notoriously jolty.
He picked up the habit in Turkey,
where the whole tradition is jerky.

* * *

Because there were so many bits in
the books of Solzhenitsyn
which gave the authorities pain,
they put him on a 'plane.

* * *

I am not too keen
on Soutine.
I think that most of his carcases
are only fit for the Marcoses.

* * *

Sir Stephen Spender
was never a gender-bender,
but in his tender way
he thought continually of those who were truly gay.

* * *

At dinner, the Dean (Dr Spooner)
mused that perhaps he would sooner
be eating the previous dish.
This was his half-warmed fish.

* * *

Gertrude Stein,
when offered a penny a line,
further expanded her prose
and wrote: 'A rose is a rose is a rose is a rose.'

* * *

Dr Marie Stopes
did a lot of research into soaps,
watching *Neighbours* and *Eastenders,*
closely observing the genders.

* * *

Once, on holiday, Lytton Strachey's
indifference to his aitches
sent Carrington straight to an arbour
when he'd meant her to wait at the harbour.

* * *

When the Romans asked Sulla
to declare his Party colour
and he answered, 'Parlour pink',
they all went home to think.

* * *

When, at Heaven's gates, St Swithin
knocked and enquired within,
he was told, 'St Peter regrets
we're not taking any more wets.'

*
* *

T

The terms in which Tacitus
castigated the Germans were acetous.
He berated them in the *Annals*
for never changing their flannels.

* * *

Sir Rabindranath Tagore
had such a splendid name, and was never a bore.
He once went on a most stimulating safari
with Mr Chakravarti Rajagopalachari.*

* * *

Thomas Tallis
loathed *Dynasty* and *Dallas*.
Soap operas, he said, were just words,
and strictly for the Byrds.

* * *

President Zachary Taylor
addressed the American nation through a loud-hailer.
As a mass-communicator he was tireless,
and they'd not yet invented the wireless.

* * *

When Terence
confessed to his parents
that he wrote humorous plays,
they disowned him, and refused to feed him for days.

* * *

* Later to be Governor-General of India (1948–50).

St Teresa
didn't care for the Mona Lisa.
She declared that a pregnant smile
was not her style.

* * *

When Valentina Tereshkova
in her Vostok 6 spacecraft flew over,
Nikita Khrushchev only half-heartedly backed her.
He considered a woman's place was on the tractor.

* * *

'Get thee to a knackery!'
cried William Makepeace Thackeray.
It was just his little jest
intended as a hint to an overstaying guest.

* * *

Mrs Thatcher *
admired Mr Gorbachev's dacha.
It quite convinced her that Chequers
was only fit for the wreckers.

* * *

* Now Baroness Thatcher of Kesteven.

There definitely was an aura
about the Empress Theodora.
Such, at least, was the opinion
of the Emperor Justinian.

* * *

'Now, you sit at ease,'
said Thucydides,
'and I'll tell you some more
about the Peloponnesian War.'

* * *

Tiberius
was quite serious
in thinking himself as august as
Augustus.

* * *

Tiglath-pileser
was a sort of Assyrian Caesar.
He supported an English mistress, Mrs Miniver,
in Nineveh.

* * *

Tintoretto
threatened with a stiletto
a man who was rather too scathing
about *Susanna Bathing*.

* * *

Toscanini
was a bottled genie.
When he got to New York
he popped the cork.

* * *

'Sweet are the uses
of Violet Trefusis,'
V. Sackville-West
would gladly attest.

* * *

When Archbishop Tutu
was shot down over the Transvaal in a U2,
countless Afrikaners
went bananas.

*
* *

U

Pope Urban
wore a tiara, not a turban.
He thought he had it made
when he launched the First Crusade.

* * *

I find it both unseemly and unamusing of
Sir Peter Ustinov
to send up poor President Reagan.*
Such 'humour' suggests the lowly mind of a pagan.

*
* *

* President Ronald Reagan (q.v.)

V

Of course, one knows that Sir John Vanbrugh
designed Canberra;
but was it he or Shaw
who wrote *What the Butler Saw* ?

* * *

Commodore Vanderbilt
had a veranda built
where he could sit in the dry
and watch his trains go by.

* * *

The French view of Vespasian
is Rabelaisian.
To think that a deified Caesar's fame should be
perpetuated in a streetside wc! *

* * *

* In Paris, street urinals were called *vespasiennes* after the emperor who, to raise new taxes, imposed the custom of 'spending a denarius'.

In her Journal for 1870, Queen Victoria
observed: 'We were moved to a state of joyous euphoria
when dear Mr Disraeli, passing on top of an omnibus,
loyally stood for the playing of God save Our Gracious Us !'

* * *

Gore Vidal
had a tendency to snarl
before the success of *Burr*.
Thenceforth he began to purr.

* * *

As Alessandro Volta
was standing at the altar,
he dreamed of domestic felicity -
complete with electricity!

*
* *

W

All letters of Lech Walesa's
are opened by the censors,
hoping to intercept dope
intended for the Pope.

* * *

Edmund Waller
got very hot under the collar
when 'Go, Lovely Rose'
appeared in a collection of English Prose.

* * *

Andy Warhol
drilled a borehole,
and let out a thrilling whoop
when it spouted Campbell's soup.

* * *

The late Earl Warren
was American, i.e. foreign.
They say he used to fret
at being less high-born than King C. Gillette.

* * *

Mr Auberon Waugh*
deplored the checkouts at his modern superstore.
Although they *scanned* correctly every time,
the items on the dockets didn't *rhyme*.

* * *

Orson Welles
liked dating awesome belles.
If a belle was *too* awesome
he'd try to arrange a foursome.

* * *

Charles Wesley
didn't dig Elvis Presley.
He would rather have gone to Hell
than written 'Heartbreak Hotel'.

* * *

* As editor of the *Literary Review* he declines to publish verse which fails to rhyme and scan.

Dame Rebecca West
was able to suggest
a few discreet hotels
to H.G.Wells.

* * *

Walt Whitman
took shorthand from Pitman,
but decided he'd travel lighter
without a typewriter.

* * *

Sir Frank Whittle
couldn't stand tittle-
tattle about the jet
set.

* * *

William of Orange
was stingy with his florins.
When throwing State banquets and such,
he insisted on going Dutch.

* * *

Though I don't mind Mr Wilson*
getting his beer from Pilsen,
I should like to know why his tobacco
comes from Cracow.

* * *

In Japan, the Duke of Windsor
could not stay away from the Ginza.
He called his favourite geisha
the Wallis Simpson of Asia.

* * *

When clergymen questioned Wordsworth
as to a bird's worth,**
the venerable bard
just hummed and hah'd.

*
* *

* Now Lord Wilson of Rievaulx.

** Cf. Are not two sparrows sold for a farthing? – Matt. 10:29.
Are not five sparrows sold for two farthings? – Luke 12:6.

X

When his wife Xanthippe
decamped with a hippy,
Socrates took the loss of her
like a philosopher.

* * *

It was deuced hard to get Xenophon
to answer the telephone.
In fact, not more than one or two such cases
are recorded in the *Anabasis*.

* * *

'Give me,' said King Xerxes,
'the man that shirks ease!'
Then he led his Persians
on strenuous excursions.

*
* *

Y

In India, Sheikh Yamani
was thus rebuked by a rani:
'*Sheikh!* Say nothing more of crude oil, if you don't mind.
It is *not* refined.'

* * *

Life was idyllic among
the disciples of Brigham Young
till Congress ordered the Mormons
to do something about their hormones.

*
* *

Z

In a bedroom where Dr Zamenhof
(with all his garments off)
was locked in his own portmanteau,
he invented Desperanto.

* * *

Emiliano Zapata
killed his inamorata
because he caught her tossing a tortilla
with Pancho Villa.

* * *

One morning when Emil Zátopek
abstractedly gave the cat a peck
instead of his lovely wife,
he had to run for his life.

* * *

Émile Zola
never wrote a word about Angola.
It was in writing of Mozambique
that he reached his peak.

* * *

Should you never have come across Richard Adolf Zsigmondy,
do not despond. He
is no longer alive.
But he happened to win the Nobel Prize for Chemistry in 1925.*

* * *

The theologian Zwingli,
soberly and succinctly,
brings this work, in all its profusion,
to a wholesome conclusion.

*

* *

* For his work on colloidal particles.

Index of Topics, Viewpoints, Qualities, Idiosyncrasies and Special Interests

CANTERBURY, See of, greater confidence in its first incumbent than in that felt for an earlier bishop of Hippo (St Augustine).

CAP, cloth, egalitarian insistence on wearing a (Popper).

CATCH PHRASES, amiable, detestation of (Jeremiah).

CATERING INDUSTRY, forced employment in the (Aesop).

CATS, male, psychological problems of, caused by neutering (Oedipus).

CAVELLERIA RUSTICANA, probable resentment at being too closely identified and even confused with the composer of (Leoncavallo).

CHAUVINISM (Foch, Ivan the Terrible); male (Akhenaten, Dior, Tereshkova).

CHEESECAKE, absolute horror of women defined as (Polk).

CHEMISTRY, Nobel Prize for (Zsigmondy).

CLAIRVOYANCE, questionable gifts of (Orwell).

CLASS-CONSCIOUSNESS (Warren).

CLERIHEWS, optimistic predisposition to savour (Lewis).

CLIMATE as an underlying factor in theological error (Erasmus); of the Iberian Peninsula (Isabella); of Northern Italy, severe winter, disturbing effects of the (Lippi).

COMMERCIALISM, successful (Milne, Schiaparelli, Stein); unsuccessful (Helen of Troy).

CONVERSATION, careless, risks of indulging in (Eve).

CONVIVIALITY (Charlemagne).

COURSE, the preferred, indecisiveness as to (Spooner).

COUTURE, HAUTE (Madariaga, Schiaparelli); *moins haute* (Dior, Hengist and Horsa).

CRITICISM, over-sensitivity to (Kipling, Tintoretto).

DADDY, SUGAR, total disinclination to be a (Polk).

SPORTS, water, military application of (Radetzky); winter, anxiety at finding oneself in proximity to an amateur of (Carey).

SPREAD, middle-aged (Byron).

STORYTELLING (Aesop, Alcott, Goebbels, Jonah, Thucydides).

SUFFERING, physical, as a goad to creative effort (Aquinas, Britten).

SUMO WRESTLERS, admiration for the physique of (the Prince Regent).

SUPERMARKET checkouts, limitations of (Waugh); promotions encouraging overspending, susceptibility to (Offa); shopping, convenience of (Giotto).

SUPERSTITION, not altogether unreasonable (Dali).

SURVIVAL, the art and architecture of (El Greco); the daily struggle for (Chanel).

TACITURNITY (Rossini).

TALKIES, speechlessness when the movies became the (Polk).

TARZAN FILMS, deplorable influence of (Santayana).

TAXIS as a safer alternative to chariots (Jezebel).

TEDIUM, capacity for enduring (the Cabots).

TENNIS (Lamartine).

THING, his own, attempt to deny a citizen's right to do (Polk).

TIBET, the impact on English chamber music of (Bax).

TIERRA DEL FUEGO, inflation of the expanse of (Mercator).

TIME, THE BIG, displeasure at seeing anyone making (Polk).

TOLERATION, religious (Piggott).

TOURISM, earnestly purposeful (Kropotkin).

TRAIN-SPOTTING (Vanderbilt).

TRANQUILITY, emotion misrecollected in (Landor).

TRANSACTIONS, commercial, vagueness with respect to (Wordsworth).

WORKHOUSE, determination not to end up in the (Chanel).

WORKS, THE, anguish at seeing even his enemies given (Polk).

WOW!, the exclamation, strong distaste for (Polk).

YIPPEE!, the exclamation, yet stronger distaste for (Polk).

ZEALOTRY, anti-beatnik (Lee Kuan Yew); Parnassian, traditionalist (Waugh).

ZIP FASTENER, the, genesis of (Agrippa).

ZO, the useful word, amazement at its point-scoring potential in Scrabble (Rabelais).

ZONKED, wrathfulness when half his cabinet turned up (Polk).

ZOOPHILIA, unhealthy tendencies to (Mahler, Mies van der Rohe).

ZOOT SUIT, sudden death when his tailor suggested he be measured for a (Polk).